# TABLE OF CONTE

1 Forward ...............................
2 Brutal beginnings.................................................. 5
3 Perception, action + will...................................... 10
4 Change your beliefs revolutionise your athleticism............. 12
5 What if I'm wrong?.............................................. 14
6 Become the listener............................................ 15
7 Get In Bed With The Devil .................................... 16
8 Embrace hardship................................................17
9 5 Ways the Ancient Romans Would Be Better At CrossFit .. 18
Than You............................................................. 18
10 Intensity is an illusion ....................................... 23
11 An introduction to intensity............................... 25
12 Teaching yourself intensity with 3 letters + a savage's tool kit................................................................. 26
13 5 WODs to test your intensity tolerance ............................. 29
14 A note on suffering .......................................... 31
15 Further reading ............................................... 33

*"In man creature and creator are united: in man there is material, fragment, excess, clay, dirt, nonsense, chaos; but there is also the creator, the sculptor, the hardness of the hammer, the divinity of the spectator, and the seventh day – do you understand this contrast? The body must be fashioned, bruised, forged, stretched, roasted, and refined – it is meant to suffer."*

- Friedrich Wilhelm Nietzsche

# 1 Forward

This book is a plea to you to work harder. It is a manual to fortifying your mind. It is a documentation of the best part of a decade obsessing over what goes on in my mind.

Because I see what happens in athletes' minds. How they defeat themselves without knowing it.

And I know how it feels. I know what it does to your selfconfidence.

I want this to plant the seed of possibility in your mind. Just as these lessons have done for me.

The book is not long: it should not detract from your time in the box.

Just as I asked my clients in my in person coaching days, I am now asking for just two more things from you: effort and trust.

Trust me that these simple methods work, give them your full effort, do not give in, and they will reward you with a fortress of a mind.

T

**THIS BOOK IS DEDICATED TO THE WOMAN THAT HAS SUPPORTED ME, KEPT ME SANE AND NEVER STOPPED BELIEVING.**

X

## 2 Brutal Beginnings

***"IT IS THE POWER OF THE MIND TO BE UNCONQUERABLE."***
Seneca

The plastic heels of my ill-fitting boots were tearing into my soft, weak, tissue. I could feel the blood starting to trickle down into my borrowed socks. I looked up into the rainy, grey sky in the South-West of England and fought back a tear as I dragged the flaccid body of Chris up the hill.

My legs were screaming for rest. I couldn't feel my hands. Above the screaming of the training team, I could hear the thumping of my heart in my ears. I couldn't see straight and the smell of drying blood that caked my nose and face was surpassingly reassuring...

We were performing what seemed like the hundredth set of backwards drags up the steepest incline in the training area. With your oppo (friend) facing away from you, you thread your arms between his arms and his body, grasp your own hands in front of his chest, then run backwards, dragging your oppo up the hill whilst he remained relaxed.

We had run, walked, crawled and duck-walked most of the infamous endurance course at this point and were soaking wet, covered in the bright orange mud of Woodbury Common and delirious with fatigue.

At that point, I'd been awake for the best part of 72 hours. I had been thrashed to the point of exhaustion. Then beyond it. My will power had been tested

I wasn't strong enough and I couldn't do this. I was just a skinny, bullied kid from a humble home who thought he could change himself.

Well I couldn't. I was going to quit.

The dream of my life for the last 5 years had been to defy all odds and prove to the world (and to myself) that I had what it took to be a Royal Marines Commando. To feel the pride when a green beret, the reward for completion of the most gruelling basic military training in the world, was placed on my head. To go back to my family and show them how I had become a man. And to finally prove to myself that I could be the man I wanted to be.

But I was going to fail. I just had nothing left to give, physically and emotionally. I was empty.

I hadn't even got accepted into training, this was just the notorious Potential Royal Marines Course.

I pictured how it would feel to come back to my girlfriend and tell her that I wasn't the man she thought I was, and at that point I was okay with it. I pictured telling the training team I had had enough. I felt the disappointment already.

And I told myself, when I got to the top of the hill, I would tell the corporal that I was quitting. I stood tall, drove my heels into the ground and waddled, one step at a time. Wading through not only the knee deep mud, but fatigue and hatred for my weakness, to the patch of grass where I would never forgive myself.

I got to the top of the hill, placed Chris down in the mud, turned to walk to the corporal and then it hit me:

*I had nothing left. Nothing. And yet I gave more.*

*"I WILL PERSIST UNTIL I SUCCEED. ALWAYS WILL I TAKE ANOTHER STEP. IF THAT IS OF NO AVAIL I WILL TAKE ANOTHER, AND YET ANOTHER. IN TRUTH, ONE STEP AT A TIME IS NOT TOO DIFFICULT.... I KNOW THAT SMALL ATTEMPTS, REPEATED, WILL COMPLETE ANY UNDERTAKING I WILL PERSIST UNTIL I SUCCEED."*
-Og Mandino

What I learnt in that moment, is that mental toughness is nothing more than a choice. I didn't know it at the time, but that started a decade long (and counting) fascination with cultivating fortitude and resilience.

For some reason, I was always happy to give in. To give in to peer-pressure, to give in to fear, to give-in to weakness. I didn't have the fight in me, and I presumed I never would.

I thought the beliefs we possess are unchangeable. That we play with the hand we are dealt. In that moment, I learned that, with skill and practise, I could reach into that deck of cards, and choose the ones that served me best.

You see, fortitude is a skill. Resilience is a skill. Being the man/woman and athlete you want to be, is a skill.

That lesson stayed with me over the course of the next 2 years as I fought my personal demons and came out of the other side with the green beret of a Royal Marines Commando on my head, the words emblazoned on my uniform, and most importantly, *an unshakeable belief that I was in control of how hard I pushed.* And therefore any successes and failures I experience are **almost entirely in my control**.

That belief and that introduction to intensity would shape the man I have become.

*1 The prize - 100% worth it*

# 3 PERCEPTION, ACTION + WILL

***"WARRIORS SHOULD SUFFER THEIR PAIN SILENTLY."***
Erin hunter

Until that moment, I lacked willpower. Well, that's what most people would say anyway. In fact, even the stoics (my heroes) would say I was lacking the third part of their philosophy. There are three parts to succeeding in any quest according to the stoics: perception, action and will.

In the view of the stoics, I had seen the situation I was in clearly and knew where I was going (perception); I had put my name down and turned up (action); all I needed was the will power to take me through. If I had given up, it would simply have been a lack of will power.

But here is what really happened, I had been through perception and action, yes. But I had also been through will until it had been completely exhausted.

What I needed to do was start the loop again at perception, not harness more willpower.

I had hit a limit in my beliefs: I didn't believe I was capable of pushing further. I needed to change my beliefs. So, what I needed was to look at the situation I was in differently.

I needed to see the situation for what it was. I needed to see *that I was in control of my effort and therefore I was in control of the outcome.*

But what is that knowledge? That knowledge is a belief. Beliefs are the stories we tell ourselves. They can help us: "I have done this before", "I am capable", "I am strong", "I'm going to give everything I have". Or they can hinder us: "I'm not feeling it today", "I suck at front squats", "what will the people watching think?", "I'm not good enough".

I cannot say this enough: your beliefs are your biggest limitations as an athlete.

It follows then, that the objective is to change our beliefs...

# 4   Change your beliefs Revolutionise your athleticism

*"CHARACTER CANNOT BE DEVELOPED IN EASE AND QUIET. ONLY THROUGH EXPERIENCE OF TRIAL AND SUFFERING CAN THE SOUL BE STRENGTHENED, AMBITION INSPIRED, AND SUCCESS ACHIEVED"* Helen Keller

When was that last time you had the experience where you looked at a barbell, thought "that's too heavy, but fuck it I'll give it a go anyway", then pulled/jerked/snatched/ benched it for a 10, 20, 30lb PR?

In the rest of this book, we will begin the process of changing those beliefs.

But for now, take a moment to think about how different your life would be if you hadn't had that belief. How much more volume could you have handled? How much confidence would you have had in a WOD? When things got tough, you could have rationalised you were only lifting 45% of your best instead of 55%.

Just changing this one thought, could have leap-frogged your performance by weeks if not months.

This belief, was a **limiting belief**.

Back to our example... All of a sudden, you have to reassess that belief. "I can't lift that" becomes "I can lift that".

So what happened?

Your actions changed your belief. This may sound like a dichotomy: you need to change your actions to change your beliefs, but you need to change your beliefs in order to change your actions.

This seems like a never ending cycle, but there's one question you need to ask yourself over and over when you hear your limiting beliefs...

# 5  What if I'm wrong?

***"THERE IS NO GOOD OR BAD WITHOUT US, THERE IS ONLY PERCEPTION. THERE IS THE EVENT ITSELF AND THE STORY WE TELL OURSELVES ABOUT WHAT IT MEANS."*** Ryan Holiday

What if everything you think isn't true? I mean, if it's happened in the past, it's certainly possible in the future, no?

Asking yourself this question is discovering a truth commonly known as a growth mindset. I won't beat the shit out of this, but a growth mindset is this "my abilities and thoughts are changeable". A growth mindset opposes a fixed mindset which sounds like this "my abilities and thoughts are unchangeable".

You hear this in kids the whole time "I'm not very good at maths", "my brother is better than me", "I'm not the smart one of our family".

You hear them mostly in kids, not adults because we have internalised them by this point. They become our narrative whether we're conscious of it or not.

As humans, we crave a certain amount of certainty, so admitting this to yourself requires first putting your ego to one side. Once we have done this, we can…

# 6 Become the Listener

---

***"THE UNIVERSE IS CHANGE. OUR LIVES ARE WHAT OUR THOUGHTS MAKE IT"*** Marcus Aurelius

1.  Listen to what you tell yourself when things get tough. Listen what you tell yourself when things are easy. When you're training, when you're thinking about training, when you're doing something completely non-related to training. Write that shit down without judgement.

2.  Start journaling. Sounds bullshitty, but its e-fucking-ssential if you ever want to master what's going on between your ears, eliminate your limiting beliefs and reach your athletic potential. Find somewhere quiet. Do not judge what you say. Do not censor yourself. Write down your feelings on a daily basis.

3.  Listen to the words you use when speaking to others about training. What we say out of habit sometimes is just that, a habit. But it has its roots in our beliefs.

# 7 GET IN BED WITH THE DEVIL

***"WHAT WE FEAR DOING MOST IS USUALLY WHAT WE MOST NEED TO DO."*** Tim Ferriss

**Our ability to endure discomfort is simply a case of familiarity.**

The phrases "get comfortable being uncomfortable" and "get uncomfortable being comfortable" have stuck around not just because of their literary elegance, but because of their usefulness.

I guarantee those that reach the CrossFit Games, or who win ultramarathons aren't experiencing discomfort for the first time when it matters.

There's a maxim in the military: "train hard, fight easy". If you are used to sucking up the hardship, gritting your teeth and fighting, you aren't going to panic when it happens in a realworld or high-stake situation.

Mental fortitude is nothing more than a familiarity with intensity.

Mental fortitude is an attribute to develop. And just in the same way that you learn to snatch, row and kip, you have to apply the same patience and dedication to building a fortress of a mind.

# 8 Embrace hardship

***"FOR IT IS NOT DEATH OR HARDSHIP THAT IS A FEARFUL THING, BUT THE FEAR OF DEATH AND HARDSHIP"*** Epictetus

In one of my more self-indulgent moments, I developed the Alpha Movement Philosophies. The second philosophy of the alpha movement describes the point above: embrace hardship.

*"Au milieu de l'hiver, j'apprenais enfin qu'il y avait en moi un été invincible."* - Albert Camus

*"In the midst of winter, I learned finally there was an unbreakable summer within me"* - Albert Camus

Comfort is often mistaken for happiness though hardship is the mother of our fortitude and our persistence.

By actively seeking out and embracing toils and struggles, we better ourselves. We become accustomed to being tough - being men.

We will never attain greatness without suffering. Without fearing. Without sleepless nights, pain and grit.

Hardship is not a surmountable obstacle on the route to success. It is the route to success.

If the destination is continuous improvement, then hardship is the map.

Grit your teeth, dig deep and suffer with joy: this is the hallmark of the greats.

# 9 5 Ways the Ancient Romans Would Be Better At CrossFit Than You

*"LOOK WELL INTO THYSELF; THERE IS A SOURCE OF STRENGTH WHICH WILL ALWAYS SPRING UP IF THOU WILT ALWAYS LOOK."* Marcus Aurelius

As we've already discussed, the ability to endure intensity is not a new discovery. It is an ability that has been round for thousands, if not hundreds of thousands of years.

In fact, I would argue that we are losing the ability to tolerate intensity. We are becoming weak and vulnerable. Our only hope is to learn from the tested practises and abandon comfort.

In ancient Rome, there were three men who embodied intensity tolerance. The lessons they taught are more applicable now than ever. They are called the Stoics.

When the average man hears the word "philosophy", his eyes glaze over. To be honest with you, I'm the same when it's presented in a way that is utterly fucking dull: you know... Old bloke with a shit beard, turtleneck and finger-print covered specs waffling on about the differences and similarities between Confucianism and Zen Buddhism.

Yeah... Not exactly exhilarating.

Until you realise that the Emperor or Rome has written you exact directions on how to crush WODs and banish weakness from your mind.

These aren't presented in a tedious way. They are easy to read and applicable to every single aspect of your life. Tim Ferriss has called Stoicism "an operating system for your mind". Just as your iPhone runs OS, your mind has the ability to utilise stoicism to make better decisions which give you the opportunity to make the most of your training.

##### LESSON #1: PRACTISE VOLUNTARY DISCOMFORT

What becomes frequent becomes the norm. What becomes the norm creates the illusion of safety.

Just as Albert Camus pointed out when talking about winter and summer earlier in this book, the stoics had their own thoughts on the best practise to achieve tolerance of adversity. The benefits of experiencing discomfort are twofold:

First, as we've mentioned, you gain familiarity. Second, you get the physical benefits of getting uncomfortable.

Putting it into practise: this one is simple. Perform the WODs detailed at the end of this book with maximal intensity.

##### LESSON #2: SEE THE SITUATION OBJECTIVELY

When you're putting lesson #1 into practise, you will want to give in. When this happens remind yourself of this: you are just a man exercising. You are trying to get better and intensity is the route to bettering yourself.

It's that simple.

When we start to cast our opinion on our actions that is when weakness rears its head. You have your goal, you have your method. You will execute that method to the best of your ability.

When you have your objective in front of you, your only responsibility in that moment is to finish it. Push that sled from A to B, not slow down for the next 3 minutes. Do not take it easy.

**Putting it into practise: create a mantra and repeat it to yourself when times get hard. Mine is *"take the path unfamiliar to others".***

LESSON #3: ALL WE HAVE IS OUR ABILITY TO CHOOSE THE RIGHT PATH

Take a moment to appreciate what you are in control of.

Your competition? No. Your thinking has no bearing on their performance. The temperature? No. So what's the point of worrying about it? The last rep? No, that has been and gone. Last time you snatched? That too has passed.

You are not in control of what has happened in the past.

Are you in control of how well your team will do? Are you in control of how you will feel after? Are you in control of the next WOD? Are you in control of what the judges will do? No.

You are not in control of what will happen in the future. So stop wasting your time and energy on what is beyond your influence.

If you can't control any of that, what can you control? Just one thing: the choices you make. More specifically, the choice you are making right this moment. Not a second from now, not a second ago, now.

So choose the path which leads to success. Are you choosing safety? Or are you choosing ceaseless effort? Are you choosing to be weak? Or to be strong?

Putting it into practise: internalise this concept. Keep it at the front of mind. Be aware of the choice you are making in this moment. Remain present. The WOD isn't a chance to switch off and escape. The WOD is a chance to connect with your best self.

LESSON #4: NEGATIVE VISUALISATION

In a world of positive thinking, unbridled optimism and "x ways to y" articles, a man is dragged into thinking that the path he chooses will be unhindered. So when he happens upon an obstacle he is flummoxed.

*Learn to plan effectively. Consider what could realistically go wrong?*

Have you ever performed a WOD then thought "if I did that again, I would never do x again"? You have, right?

So why not practise it internally first, feel it before "3, 2, 1 go", visualise the movements, know it inside and out. This way you will discover your path before you have started. Think of every single thing that could go wrong. Shoelaces coming undone, collars breaking, arms being blown out.

Putting it into practise: when warming up, integrate an indepth visualisation of the WOD to come. See not only what will go wrong, but what you will do to combat it and still crush it.

LESSON #5: OBSTACLES = OPPORTUNITIES

**"THE IMPEDIMENT TO ACTION ADVANCES ACTION. WHAT STANDS IN THE WAY BECOMES THE WAY"** - Marcus Aurelius.

Intensity sucks… If you aren't going to greet it with enthusiasm. Because it is hard, you should accept it into your world. Not just accept it, but love it.

When confronted with an obstacle we can either expend crucial energy getting around it, or we can expend less energy smashing straight through the middle of it.

Putting it into practise: what are your biggest fears in your training? Write them out. Learn the principles behind the people who are best at your weaknesses. Learn their method. Execute it.

# 10 Intensity is an Illusion

***"FOCUS ON THE MOMENT, NOT THE MONSTERS THAT MAY OR MAY NOT BE UP AHEAD."*** Ryan Holiday

One of the biggest and cognitively demanding interviews I have ever done on The Alpha Movement Podcast... but I couldn't concentrate on conversation with sleep genius, Doctor Kirk Parsley. Worse than that, all I could focus on was my dry mouth, the cold sweat covering my body and the taste/smell of vomit.

45 minutes before, I thought it was a good idea to hit 50 calories for time on the assault bike. The thought process I had was this: 1-2 minutes of pain, 3-5 minutes of catching my breath, 10 minutes of mobility, 5 minute jog home, 5 minute shower, begin the interview.

But it went more like this: 1-2 minutes of balls out effort, 30 minutes of being sick into a child's play bucket and trying to regain my vision, a 10 minute stumble home whilst vomiting again, set up microphone and hit record.

This was one of the most intense workouts I have ever experienced and it all began with one thought: ***"intensity is an illusion".***

As survival machines, human beings are hard-wired to avoid non-essential effort. We naturally want to conserve as much energy as possible. I'd been reading a book on human evolution and this point really stuck in my mind.

I started to question myself... if intensity was a trick designed to stop us expending too much energy unnecessarily, was it possible that limit has been downregulated too far?

What's more, is it possible to overwhelm this safety-guard with mental fortitude?

The answer: yes.

# 11 An Introduction to Intensity

---

***"WHAT IS TO GIVE LIGHT MUST ENDURE BURNING."*** Viktor Frankl

Now, you may have heard that when people push too hard they break themselves. You'd be correct in that assumption, but only when they don't understand the difference between intensity and pain.

This is a lesson Julien Pineau taught me on The Alpha Movement Podcast and in Strong Fit's *truly excellent seminars*. **Intensity is safe, pain is not.**

Basically, what we're looking for is subjective. Does it feel sketchy or just hard? Are you clicking, popping, feeling hotspots erupt around your joints? Or can you just feel the burn?

If you follow the Weight-bearing – Eccentric - Skill principle, you are more than likely going to remain strong in your pursuit of intensity.

Once we learn to identify this difference, we can throw ourselves into the WODs.

# 12 Teaching yourself intensity with 3 letters + a savage's tool kit

*"STRENGTH IS THE PRODUCT OF STRUGGLE. YOU MUST DO WHAT OTHERS DON'T TO GET WHAT OTHERS WON'T"*
Henry Rollins

### Skill eccentric weight-bearing

The more skill a movement requires, the more eccentric loading the more weight your structure bears, the less intensity you can experience.

That's why heavy Isabel (30 snatches for time at 100kg or 225lbs) is such a hard WOD; it requires huge neural capacity, have to have to perform a fair amount of eccentric control and we have to support a lot of weight

Note: skill, eccentric loading, and weight bearing movements in themselves are not bad in themselves, but when we are trying to experience intensity, they limit our ability to experience new limits.

The aim therefore, if we're trying to teach you intensity, is to find exercises that require very little skill or eccentric phases and have minimal structural loading.

We need to find movements and wods whose output will never be limited by potential danger or complexity. The following kit can be used in a way that the only thing limiting you is your mind.

When you use these, it's never because it's too complex, or because your loading eccentrically or because you're supporting a lot of outside weight on your structure, but because you give in.

This is what we want, tools to train your intensity tolerance.

### ASSAULT BIKE

The devil's tricycle. If you've used one of these, you'll know how much they suck. Get aggressive and it gives back more than you can throw at it.

Skill: next to none, just cycle and throw your hands back and forth whilst pedalling. Eccentric: minimal if any weight bearing: none

One caveat: set up your saddle correctly.

### PROWLER/SLED

This is the tool to train intensity tolerance. Elegant in design and use, it has no real equal.

Skill: if you have even barely functioning legs, you can use this

(next to none) eccentric loading: none weight bearing: none

How to use:

Push, pull, drag. Attach many different harnesses/ropes to add variety

### WATT BIKE

A close rival to the Assault Bike, but comes in second because of its slightly higher skill requirement and lack of upper body involvement.

Skill: some - it helps it you're a good cyclist eccentric loading: very little you can work hard here! Weight bearing: none

This is kind of a last resort, along with a concept 2 rowing machine. Both require some decent technique to get the most out of them.

SANDBAGS

Ah, the real beast. Humbling and elegant, sandbags will make a warrior out of you. As unforgiving as they are effective, sandbags are one of my favourite tools to induce Intensity Tolerance.

Skill: Fair. But it's brutally outweighs it. Also, due to its natural loading patterns (in comparison to a barbell), your body usually adapts to force fairly good movement and torque.

How to use: carry it, put it over your head, squat it, clean and jerk it, chuck it over your shoulder, deadlift it... whatever you do with a barbell, transfer it over to the sandbag.

If you are going to buy sandbags, there is only one place to go: Strong Fit (https://www.strongfit.com/product-page/sand-bag)

# 13 5 WODS TO TEST YOUR INTENSITY TOLERANCE

*"... THE PERSON IN TRAINING MUST SEEK TO RISE ABOVE, SO AS TO STOP SEEKING OUT PLEASURE AND STEERING AWAY FROM PAIN"* Musonius Rufus

INTENSITY TOLERANCE WOD #1:

For time:

Airbike: 50 calories

As pat sherwood would say, this wod is brutally elegant. Void of complexity, it allows you to experience your true limits then smash through them.

INTENSITY TOLERANCE WOD #2

For time: 800m prowler push @ bodyweight x1.25 (scale weight if necessary) rest 5 minutes repeat once more

The aim is to keep the sled moving for the entire 800m. Do not stop moving. The only thing stopping you is your mind.

INTENSITY TOLERANCE WOD #3 2

rounds for time:

200m sled rope pull hand over hand @ 60% of bodyweight
20 calories on the airbike

INTENSITY TOLERANCE WOD #4

On assault bike: find your maximal power output. Rest until fully recovered (5-10 minutes).

Maintain at least 75% of that power output for as long as possible. You have three "lives" you lose a life every time you go under 75%

INTENSITY TOLERANCE WOD #5

The prowler bleep test

Start a running clock every 30 seconds, push the prowler 20m/60ft add 5kg every 1:00

Start with @20kg on the prowler

# 14 A NOTE ON SUFFERING

***"THERE IS ONLY ONE WAY TO HAPPINESS AND THAT IS TO CEASE WORRYING ABOUT THINGS WHICH ARE BEYOND THE POWER OF OUR WILL."*** Epictetus

When you think back to the most awful things that have happened to humans, the slaughter of innocents in WWII is up there.

To take a detour into a grim territory, imagine being starved, abused, watching your family being executed, worked to the bone and a whole lot more. How any man could come out of that situation sane, let alone positive leaves me speechless.

Yet many did. One of those was psychiatrist, author and philosopher, Viktor Frankl.

In his beautiful book *Man's Search For Meaning*, Frankl talks about the suffering he went through. He talks of the most disgusting treatment and how he learned to cope.

At one point, he hasn't eaten in days, possibly weeks, has been working on the railroads in freezing conditions with almost no clothes and is close to death, not for the first time. He is considering ending it all, again, not for the first time.

Eventually, he is given food. His portion is a single rotting head of a fish. At that moment, he has an epiphany. He looks at the scales of the fish and sees the beauty in them. The colours and the texture. He looks up and he sees the trees and the snow and a bird.

He realises at that moment, he can see the world in two ways: in the injustices he is suffering or he can see the obvious beauty around him. He can practise gratitude for what he has or he can practise hatred.

It is a choice.

I'm not in any way putting mid-WOD suffering on the same level as Nazi oppression! But it's a sliding scale.

Hopefully it won't take something this appalling for you to realise what is inherently beautiful in the situation you find yourself in.

Remember, you have a choice to make right now: do you perceive pain or do you understand it's an opportunity?

***"IF THERE IS MEANING IN LIFE AT ALL, THEN THERE MUST BE A MEANING IN SUFFERING. SUFFERING IS AN INERADICABLE PART OF LIFE, EVEN AS FATE AND DEATH. WITHOUT SUFFERING ... HUMAN LIFE CANNOT BE COMPLETE."*** – Viktor Frankl

# 15 FURTHER READING

Often, a list of resources that have influenced a writer are overlooked as a frivolity. With all my sincerity though, I recommend these books, podcasts and people to anyone who wants to master their mind and perform better as both an athlete, and a human being.

BOOKS

*Meditations:* Marucs Aurelius

*The Daily Stoic*: Ryan Holiday

*The Obstacle Is The Way*: Ryan Holiday

*Ego Is The Enemy*: Ryan Holiday

*Psychocybernetics*: Maxwell Maltz

*Mindset*: Carol Dweck

*On The Shortness of Life*: Seneca the Younger

*Man's Search for Meaning*: Viktor Frankl


PEOPLE (IN ADDITION TO THE AUTHORS ABOVE)

Brian Grasso + Carrie Campbell (www.brianandcarrie.live)

Julien Pineau + Richard Aceves / StrongFit

Ben Bergeron

PODCASTS

The Tim Ferriss Show

Philosphize This!

# 16 "Secret" Chapter Only In The First 100 Copies Of This Book

*If you're reading this, the offer is still open!*

Discover How To Push Harder Than Ever, Create Habits That Stick (Mobility/Nutrition?!) And Develop Unbeatable Motivation

Apply For You Free Grit Call: email <tom@alphamovement.co> with the subject "FREE GRIT CALL"

We know WHAT to do – daily mobility, perfect nutrition, push harder. So why the hell don't we do it?

When I first started working with Adam, he had a reputation in our box as a great athlete, but in his eyes he never fulfilled his potential.

At one (very drunken) xmas party, I caught up with him and he admitted to never being able to push as hard as he wanted. He knew he *could* push harder, but always paced himself – left a bit in the tank.

He hadn't hit a PR in months and his performance in local comps was starting to suck. He lost all motivation. Started binging at the weekends (then during the weeks), completely gave up on his mobility work.

He admitted he was feeling grumpy as hell too. He'd been taking his frustration out on his girlfriend and their relationship was suffering.

"I just feel like I'll never be good enough. I ALWAYS fail." he said.

At that moment, I felt his pain. A couple of years before that, I was in exactly the same situation, down to arguing with my girlfriend.

I was, like Adam, at my wits end. I hated what I did and who I had let myself become.

But in the years between then and this conversation, I had changed myself around. Everyone in the box knew me as the "Master Motivator". I now know my limits. I LOVE to push myself to the edge and then beyond.

What happened?

I said enough was enough and in a last-ditch effort, I threw myself into learning about human motivation, psychology and habit formation. In short:

WHY DON'T PEOPLE DO THE THINGS THEY KNOW THEY SHOULD DO?

And

WHAT SEPARATES THE WINNERS FROM THE LOSERS?

I told Adam that story and thought I saw a glimmer of hope in his eyes (although it could have just been the rum).

We booked my first ever "Grit Call" for the next day.

You can do exactly the same, for free, right here: http://alphamovement.co/free-grit-call

Through our hangovers, we started to pick apart why Adam was feeling like this. I explained to him HE WAS NOT BROKEN. I showed him how capable he is.

Most importantly, I showed him the incredibly simple program I had perfected for myself. With a bit of fine-tuning, we adapted it for him (everyone is different).

I showed him the secret work I had been doing for the last 12 months in the box. I showed him my 5-minute morning routine that fires me up. I showed him everything I learned until that point.

You wouldn't believe how he has changed as an athlete (and as a man!). I spoke to him a couple of days back and I asked about his consistency of training (his biggest issue). He has missed 2 training sessions in the past 18 months!!

This is what he said: "I have never felt so good! I've almost DOUBLED my clean and jerk. My Fran time is now sub-3. Also, I placed 2nd in my local comp a few weekends back"

"But most of all, I now love the athlete I am. I've always wanted to work this hard and hated everyone else who could. Now I am the envy of the box and the other guys look up to me."

"I try to explain what I did and how it's so simple, but they don't believe me!"

Since my call with Adam, my GRIT Calls have become notorious with a small but growing number of athletes who have fulfilled their athletic potential with my teachings.

The past 12 months, I have been charging $97 for them. But now I'm giving a limited away for free.

**\*\*If you're reading this, your GRIT call is still available!\*\***

Because it's such an honour to see just how athletes transform on these calls.

You can apply for your extremely limited FREE Grit Call (Worth $97) here: email tom@alphamovement.co with the subject "FREE GRIT CALL"

As I said, I'm only giving away 10 of these, so you must apply now.

So if you are an athlete who:

\*\* struggles to push yourself hard

\*\* doesn't stick to your mobility or nutrition plan

\*\* Is ready to make simple changes

** Is an action taker

** Is ready to become a better athlete than you ever believed possible


Then this is for you.


So now is the time to be the athlete you've always dreamed of being. Apply now for your free call: email tom@alphamovement.co with the subject "FREE GRIT CALL"

Printed in Poland
by Amazon Fulfillment
Poland Sp. z o.o., Wrocław